Scattered
Heart

Scattered Heart

First published in paperback in 2014 by Write Path NI Limited.

A catalogue record for this book is available from the British Library.

ISBN 978 0 9927824 2 9

For more copies of this book, please email:
info@writepathni.com

Cover designed by Write Path NI Limited

Scattered Heart

By

Roisin Donnelly

Write Path NI Limited

About the Author

Roisin Donnelly, although born in Canada, spent her early years in Ireland before moving back to Canada to finish her education, gaining a BA in English from Brock University.

Now living in Ireland, Roisin is dedicating her time to fulfilling her dreams; working on her first novel and writing for a magazine. Although she has seen her poems published in 'Stars in Our Hearts', and 'Great Poets Across America', Scattered Heart is her first collection.

For more information on Roisin, and her work, please contact info@writepathni.com.

I would like to send a big thank you out to my mum and dad, Siobhan and John, for their unconditional love and support, and to my wonderful siblings; Blanaid, Angharad, and Fintan, for always being there for me.

Also, to the amazing Janine Cobain, and Write Path NI, thank you for taking a chance on me and seeing my potential as a writer.

Last, but not least, thank you to everyone who reads this collection of poetry; I hope that it resonates with some of your own experiences in life.

Roisin Donnelly

CONTENTS

CONTENTS

Scattered Heart

My heart shattered when you said goodbye

The pieces were scattered when you slammed the door

I lay like a rag doll, limp from trying to maintain control

I didn't even have the strength to cry

No tears would bless these cold, empty eyes

I was no longer the person you once loved

You took her with you, bundled up in memories

Now just a hollow shell of a girl I once knew

I lay there still not knowing what to do

Notes

Crying in the Rain

No one sees when you're crying in the rain
No one sees your heartache and pain
The tears, that fall from your eyes
Mix with the raindrops falling from the sky
Each drop reflects a life gone by
Memories of a wretched goodbye

Feel the weight being washed away
Of a love that wasn't meant to be
Finally, open your eyes and see
That you can now be free
No more heartache or pain
No more crying in the rain

Roisin Donnelly

Notes

Addiction

You're like an addiction

You're like a drug

You're a craving I have that I can't give up

You clear my thoughts

You calm my nerves

You're all I need to ease the hurt

There is no crying

There is no pain

When I have you coursing through my veins

I am up on a cloud

High above the world

You're the only thing that I need on this earth

You are my escape

My oasis from all

I know you'll catch me

When I fall

Notes

The Darkness

The darkness surrounds me

The walls are caving in

I am lost in this chaos

With no exit in sight

I am fumbling through the hallways

Stumbling over debris

Trying to find my way out

Trying to break free

My vision is getting blurry from the dust in the air

I am trying to get out step by step

But my strength is wavering

My legs are giving out

I am tired from fighting

I have begun to doubt

My escaping this crumbling house

I have lost the energy to scream and shout

The darkness surrounds me

The walls are caving in

I am lost in this chaos

Bury me in the dust

Roisin Donnelly

Notes

By Your Side

Staring up at the stars

Watching the world go by

I can feel that you are no longer by my side

I can make a wish upon a shooting star

Hoping it'll find you wherever you are

Wishing you well, in all that you do

Hoping you find a love that is pure, and true

Try not to forget me, as the days go by

Even though I'm no longer by your side

Notes

Grey Eyes

I saw a shadow walking at the dawn of day

As they looked to the moon their eyes reflected

A tale full of sorrow and pain

I saw a tear form in the grey eye

And was struck in awe

As it glistened and made its descent

Down the shadow's face to fall on the ground below

With a thud that echoed across the field

I was shaken to my core by the tragic and

yet beautiful scene

And gently made my exit

Before the grey eyes turned on me

Notes

Final Day

My wings have become brittle in the early frost

If I don't find shelter, all that I am will be lost

The snow has begun to fall

Swirling around me like the breaking tide

Making me frightened and running to hide

Have to find shelter to keep warm

Have to run from this whirlwind storm

I realize too late there is no where to go

My eyes search frantically but even so

As time continues to tick away

My wings begin to break and whither away

I lose strength and tremble and sway

My knees connect with the snow covered ground

And I realise in this moment I'm no longer bound

To this earth or existence

So I lift my hands up to the darkened sky

Say a prayer and close my eyes

Notes

Broken Wings

She flies through the night on broken wings

Wishing to recreate her beautiful dreams

Looking for a place to land

Looking for Mother Nature to take her hand

To save her from her agony

To restore her once upon a time glory

To dry her silent tears

And chase away her fears

She flies through the night on broken wings

Wishing to recreate her beautiful dreams

Notes

Her Song

She stands on top the Scottish moors
The girl with the red hair and green cloak
She stands and sings to the ocean
Singing in a foreign tongue
And if you get close enough you are able to see
The tears falling from her grey eyes,
Mixing into the sea
No one knows who she's singing to
No one even knows her name
But you can be sure to find her there
Always singing her song just the same

Notes

Stranger

You're not the person you use to be

I don't know this stranger

Standing in front of me

You've changed

And, I guess

So have I

But now you seem bitter and I don't know why

You asked for this

It was what you were hoping for

But now that you have it

You're still looking for more

I gave you all that I had for so long

There's nothing left of me

It's time to move on

I need to break free from your grasp

I need to let go of the past

I'm no longer the person I used to be

And I no longer know this stranger

Standing in front of me

Notes

Fairy Tale

Life doesn't read like a fairy tale
There are rips in the pages
And the spine is cracked
But I'm still hoping that I can go back
To when the days were good, and fun
And there were no worries about what was to come
I am no queen, and you are no king
Our life won't appear on the pages
Of a glossy magazine
We have to deal with what we have
We get to choose our own path
Although it won't be a fairy tale
I still get to decide that one fine detail
Of whether I live, or die
Of whether I will be happy, or will cry
I don't know how my story is going to end
But I do know I am the author
And that's a God send

Notes

You Can...

You can... cry until your heart's content
You can... pick your scabs until they bleed
You can... worry about stupid nonsense
You can... become consumed with greed
You can... wander the corridors of your soul
You can... see the canvas of your heart
You can... try to grow from your mistakes
You can... try and make a new start
You can... look towards a new dawn
You can... look towards a new day
You can... stop being a simple pawn
And learn how to master the game

Notes

Casualty

I wander around the streets at night

Looking for somewhere to rest

My eyes are getting heavy

And my legs are doing their best

To keep propelling me forward

To stop me from falling down

But each step I take seems to

Be bringing me closer to the ground

My mind has stopped working

My arms have gone limp

And I know it won't be long now

Until I'm nothing but a blimp

On this timeline they call life

In this great big universe

I'll just be another casualty

Another line, another verse

In Mother Nature's song

About the failure of this Earth

Notes

Loving Arms

When the world looks bleak and there is no sun

When the skies open up and people run

For shelter, for cover, it's all the same

No one can hide from nature's reign

She can create, she can destroy

She can dictate sadness, and joy

She rules the world, she takes control

She can leave you wandering in the cold

There is no escape, there is no way out

You just have to put faith and never doubt

She will nurture the world and protect it from harm

She will keep it always in her loving arms

Notes

Tragic Fall

You made me laugh everyday
You never cared what people would say
I was your girl and you were my man
And in our world we had the perfect plan
To grow old together through rain or shine
To love each other until the end of time
Our world soon crumpled and it fell to the ground
Outside forces tore it all down
We were exposed to the world once and for all
There was no coming back from this tragic fall
As the days grew longer so did the cold
We could no longer pretend to be bold
In the face of danger or the elements at hand
It was time to retreat we could no longer take a stand
We had begun losing faith and strength fast
We knew we wouldn't be able to recreate the past
So we looked each other in the eye
Knowing this was our final goodbye

Notes

Second Chance

I've looked to the stars for answers for so long

That I forgot what my heart feels is never wrong

I may be looking to the universe for some guidance

When I should be asking you for another chance

You're my best friend and lover too

I know that I can't survive without you

So I'm asking you for another chance

To try and recapture the romance

We used to be so in love

And I want you back my turtle dove

I will do anything to have your hand once again

I'll keep on trying until you bend

You mean so much to me in every way

I'm not going anywhere I'm here to stay

Notes

Intertwined

I sat on the pier

Watching your ship sail away

Hoping in my heart that you'll come back

One day

Although we were only together for a short time

I know that our hearts are forever

Intertwined

You loved me with no questions asked

We never had to discuss the past

We trusted each other with no doubt

That we knew each other's souls

Inside, and out

You were my sailor

And I was your maid

I wish now in my heart that you had stayed

Off the course of the seven seas

Staying at home safe with me

Notes

Nature's Reign

I stare up at the stars tonight
As they twinkle ever so bright
I never thought that I would see the day
That nature's love has come to stay
She wraps her arms around us all
And catches us when we are about to fall
Her love knows no limits or bounds
She nurtures us through the ground
By loving the earth and letting it grow
In order for us to survive the snow
In winter, fall, summer and spring
All year long I worship her Majesty the Queen

Notes

Demons

I can see straight into your heart

The inner workings of your soul

I wish I could heal all the hurt and pain

That surrounds you like the cold

The cogs and chains are wound up tight

Almost at the breaking point

I need to try and unwind them

To stop them crushing your spirit and soul

I wish I could be there

To hold your hand at night

I wish I could be there

To hold you in my arms tight

The demons haunt the corners of your mind

I am no match for their kind

I left you wide open and on display

I left you alone in your despair

I didn't have the strength to repair

All the damage that lies beneath

Those black eyes that never sleep

Notes

Numb

The winds are howling around me

The rain is falling hard

But I continue to stand here

In the dark and cold

Letting the raindrops wash over me

I don't want to be protected

I just want to feel again

I have become so numb

To the emotions and pain

I have lost all of me

In the blink of an eye

Why can't you see?

That all you do is hurt me

Notes

Hour of Need

Stay with me

In my hour of need

Please don't abandon me

We have come so far

Traveling across land and sea

You are my moon and stars

Nothing can break us apart

Please just stay with me

In this time and space

Don't break the moment

Please don't abandon me

In my hour of need

Stay with me

Notes

Buried Beneath

All you see is the light in my eyes

And the smile on my face

You don't see the scars

Buried beneath

I can't keep up with your pace

I just want to run to the darkest corner

And hide myself away from the enemy

But I can't outrun me

My mind is tired and my legs are numb

My past is finally catching up with me

My scars are no longer

Buried beneath

It's time to let go

It's time to be free

Notes

Dark Abyss

The eyes are the window to the soul

I wish I could see all that you hold

Buried deep down inside that dark place

Where no one is granted access to that space

You keep yourself locked up in everyway

Never letting anyone in to stay

To try and coax you out of yourself

To bring light to your world and wash away doubt

You want to be free I can see it in your eyes

Let me try and help you sever the ties

That hold you in that dark abyss

Let me show you living is bliss

Notes

Turning to Dust

I gave you my all, but it wasn't enough
And now I sit here with my heart turning to dust
You saw that you were destroying me,
With lies and lust
But you continued to betray my trust
I don't understand why
I continue to give you all my time
When I gain nothing as I sit here
Losing my mind
I wait for a call, or text saying 'missing you'
But my phone is blank
And no calls have come through
Why do I continue to waste my time on you?
Why do I still care about all the stuff that you do?
I need to break away to be free
I need this in order to restore my sanity

Notes

Can't Escape

I am caught

Between holding on, and letting go

My heart clings to you

With all its strength

Whereas my mind keeps trying to release the grasp

I know I should say no, and walk away

But there is a pull to you that just won't fray

I am stuck

Not knowing what to do

While all the time I just want to be with you

I don't know what my next step is supposed to be

My eyes are wide open,

But they can't see

There is a map in my hand,

But I'm still lost in this place

And there's a pull to you that I can't escape

I am caught

Between holding on, and letting go

If we are meant to be together

Then it will be so

Notes

Chasing Thoughts of You Away

I'm sitting in a dark corner

Trying to chase thoughts of you away

I can see you clearly

Like it was yesterday

That you left me confused

Wishing that you would stay

All I wanted was to feel love

But now I feel nothing at all

I try to drink away the memories

But in the light of day

They come back to me

And now I can't escape

This wasn't meant to be my fate

Sitting in a dark corner

Chasing thoughts of you away

Notes

Courage

I always hide my tears from you
I always try to be strong
I always try to play the game
Even when it's going all wrong
I always put you before me
I always say yes before no
I always want to please you
Through hail, rain and snow
I always have a smile on
I always try to understand
I always try to comfort you
I obey your every command
But I realize I can no longer stand
To live this life I lead
I need to take courage
To walk away and leave
To no longer hide my tears
To stand up to my fears

Notes

Trying To Hold On

Trying to hold on

To a life that is no longer mine

Trying to recreate a past

That ran out of time

I still want to be with you

Even though I shouldn't

I still feel like there is so much

For us to do

That we can make it work

That we can be true

I won't deny

We've had our ups and downs

Once or twice

I almost left town

But thinking of you

Made me put my guard down

I don't know if we are meant to be

But you still have all of me

And until we give this another chance

I won't know if I've taken the right stance

Notes

Sweet Kiss

I miss feeling your skin

Beneath my fingertips

I miss curling up beside you

Waiting for your sweet kiss

I miss the way you smell

And your gentle touch

I miss how you'd say 'I love you' so much

I miss your smile

And that twinkle in your eye

I miss you making me mad

I won't deny

Because at least I had you in my life

In the end it was always worth the fight

Notes

My Heart

At the sound of your voice
My heart still skips a beat
I try to keep my emotions
Under control from the heat
That comes from my ignited heart
Lit inside from your simple smile
It's like a never ending tide
Of feelings that just won't subside
My body can't handle the pain
Of never having you again
Watching you from across the room
Is all it takes to make me weak and swoon
I realize you're out of my reach
But still each night I cry myself to sleep

Notes

Terrors of the Night

Not a word was said

Just a simple smile

I knew then that you'd be gone for a while

Not sure when you'd be coming home

But I'd have to cope with being alone

With no one to talk to in an empty house

My mind started to wander

To a place of doubts

Where walls, bricks, fences the lot

Wouldn't keep out my dark thoughts

Closing my eyes only makes things worse

So sleep deprivation was my cure and curse

With heavy eyes I couldn't see sense

With a foggy mind I was spent

I didn't have the urge to fight

So I finally gave in to terrors of the night

Notes

Will I Ever

Will I ever get over you?

Will my heart ever mend?

Will I be able to walk past you in the street

And not have my legs crumble and bend

I need for you to not have this hold on me

I need to truly break free

I need to move on with my life

I need to get back to being me

Will I ever not want to kiss you goodnight

Will I ever stop feeling joy and light

When you are around me

Will my heart ever see

That you can no longer hold the key

Notes

Missing You

I lie in a bed

In a room, in a house that doesn't feel like home

I miss you cuddling me and keeping my feet warm

I miss waking up every morning and seeing your face

I miss coming home to your sweet embrace

Your kisses were like nothing

I had ever felt before

I know you've walked away

Leaving me scarred once more

I thought that my heart could take it, I really did

But three times my heart has been pushed to its limit

Everyone keeps telling me that I need to move on

But if you called tomorrow

I'd be back with you before dawn

I know I need to be strong and just let go

But I miss the man that stole my heart so

I lie in a bed

In a room, in a house that doesn't feel like home

Wishing for you

To come and save me from being alone

Notes

Without You

You were the storm

That swept me off my feet

You were the earthquake

That made my heart skip a beat

You were the volcano

That heated me to my very core

You were the hurricane

That broke down my walls

You were the ocean

That washed away all my tears

You were the sun

That chased away all my fears

The stars and planets

Revolve around you

I don't know what I would do

Without you

Notes

All That I Am

Mute

Like a Barbie doll

Fragile

As a china doll

Complicated

Like a Rubik's cube

Difficult

As a game of Clue

Fragmented

Like a jigsaw

Off balance

Like a see-saw

Ruled

By a king

Defeated

By a knight

Losing

This game and fight

Fragile

Like a china doll

Mute

Like a Barbie doll

Notes

Farewell

As I lie in the grass
Staring up at the sky
I let go of my fears and whisper goodbye
The sun shines on my face and hair
Leaving me feeling peaceful and without a care
I outstretch my arm and sweep it across the grass
And the blades tickle my palm instead of being crass
And I have a premonition that I can be happy at last
As a cloud passes over the sun I know it's time to go
Before it gets too dark for me to see my way home
I turn back towards the meadow
And for a second I stall
Looking at the beautiful sight before me
And tightening my shawl
Knowing that I'll be back soon
I say farewell to the moon

Notes

One Way Track

This has been a journey that I will never forget

My memories will remain with not an ounce of regret

As I sit on the train watching the world go by

I try to stop the tears that I cry

Knowing I won't see you again

But I loved being caught in the whirlwind

Of first love and true romance

I couldn't have asked for a better chance

To feel all the emotions swirling around in me

Walking with a beating heart that only you could see

I know my eyes will give it all away

As they reflect all the feelings

I have tried to keep at bay

I know there is no going back

As I am on this one way track

This has been a journey that I will never forget

My memories will remain, without regret

Also available from Write Path NI

Volunteer by Gary McElkerney

Chris Johnston, a 22 year old university student from Belfast, signs away another summer to lead a team of young volunteers as they travel to Ethiopia to build houses for charity. After an argument with the other leaders, Chris abandons the team and travels north to work for Medical Aid Africa in a clinic close to the Eritrean border. He agrees to join their make-shift ambulance crew in a bid to find the excitement he's been searching for on the frontline, but finds life very different off the beaten track. Consumed by fear, he is terrified and experiences the true horrors of war as his dreams of heroism and adventure turn into a nightmare. Volunteer is laced with humour, heartbreak and horror and Chris' journey will leave you questioning your own life, your achievements. If faced with the same situations, what would you do? And if the mental scars of war were carved into your memories, who would save you?